Skip Trace Secrets

Dirty little tricks skip tracers use...

By Valerie McGilvrey

Copyright © 2012, 2013, 2014 McGilvrey Publishing

Library of Congress   10 9 8 7 6 5 4 3 2 1

ISBN: 978-1-62050-376-8
ISBN-13: 978-1479350971
ISBN-10: 1479350974
Updated as to content October 15, 2013
SECOND EDITION

Disclaimer & Legal Notice:

No part of this book may be reproduced or transmitted in any form or by any means electronically or mechanically including photocopying, recording or by any information storage and retrieval system, without permission in writing from the author and publisher. Forward inquiries to McGilvrey Pub P.O. Box 1906, Montgomery, Texas 77356

Some methods of skip tracing may be illegal in your country, state, county or city. Please inquire into the law governing where you live or where you work. The use of this volume is at your own risk. This book is not legal advice; please consult with an attorney for legal issues. Complete knowledge of the FDCPA is very important to all skip tracers, repossession agents and collectors. This can be found at: www.ftc.gov/bcp/edu/pubs/consumer/credit/cre27.pdf

Background Check
by Valerie McGilvrey

A complete human resources and entrepreneur hiring guide. Learn to do your own background checks for private gun sales, small business hiring and land-lording.

Also for the concerned parent or curious dater. Includes release forms, authorization forms and outlines the Interview Method widely used by to background check agencies.

http://www.amzn.to/checkfacts

The Most Useful Websites: For Small Business & Entrepreneurs

This is a brilliant compilation of websites and a book you'll refer to often. Filled with helpful and little known inspirational sites for marketing, sales and business operations. If you're an information hound then this book is the kind of thing that you'll love.

http://www.amzn.to/mostuseful

Dirty little tricks skip tracers use...

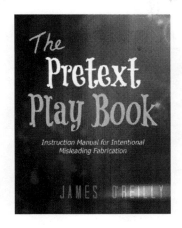

**The Pretext Play Book
by James O'Reilly**

A pretext? Surely, you jest, but they've been used by the best of the best!

The Pretext Play Book is a comprehensive guide on the investigative skill of pretexting. Not all skip tracing can be successful with traditional methods, so investigators use hacking and scams to get the information that is the target of their investigation.

Discover pretexts used by law enforcement, skip tracers, repossession and private investigators worldwide. Idea's and Social Engineering scenario's that get results and have hundreds of possibilities. Advanced techniques and modern formulas to trick even the savviest of today's absconders.

http://www.amzn.to/pretextplaybook

**How to be a Repo Man:
The Complete Repo Operation Guide**

By James O'Reilly

Vehicle repossession is a recession proof business with fast payoff. In this easy to understand guide you'll learn every angle of the business from a career repo man. Learn how to get started, get work, find people and get paid.

James O'Reilly gives specific insight into a debtor's mind for profiling and getting the repo work that no one else can get. Business building advice gives you the good reputation you need to stay in flooded in work for years to come. Cash in on a down turned economy with your own repossession agency.

http://www.amzn.to/repomanprint

Visit Valerie's online blog for contributions from around the web on investigations and skip tracing.

www.TheDailySkip.com
News skip tracers can use!

Connect with Valerie on LinkedIn:

Valerie@McGilvrey.com

Twitter me @skipease

Dedicated to Ray

Thank you for your friendship.

Table of Contents

What is a skip?...13

Introduction...14

Dissecting the Skip...16

A Good Start...18

Basic Needs...22

Be Better Than Your Best Database...29

Profiling the Skip...36

Databases...38

Free!...46

Verification...49

Making Contact...53

Professional Licensing...61

Place of Employment...63

Military Personnel...65

Bankruptcy...68

Social Media...69

Email...74

The Phone...76

Cease & Desist...84

Seasonal Skipping...85

What Do Background Searches Consist Of?...87

The Ultimate Skip Trace List...89

Marketing...96

*When you make your personal business public,
The public makes you their personal business.*

What is a skip?

Skip tracing is the investigative method of locating missing people. Skipped town, skipping out, and skipping on are all skip lingo and that means someone has moved on and by doing so someone else got the shaft, stiffed and stuck with the bill.

In this book, I refer to the subject that you are looking for as a debtor. The person that has skipped could be called your subject, escaped convict, bond jumper, deadbeat parent, suspect, or cheater. Relatively all the same, for whatever reason it may be, you're still looking for someone who doesn't want to be found.

Skip tracing efforts are not just for locating someone either. Skip tracing can also be used to verify the accuracy of the debtor's information in the process of determining credit worthiness in your small business. Pre-employment screening and background searches for other legal transactions need skip trace efforts to confirm a standard of ethics for a hiring company.

Who needs a skip tracer? A wide array of professional positions need skip tracers or need to have people locating skills. Attorneys, process servers, investigators, law enforcement, reporters, realtors, bounty hunters, bail bonds agencies, debt collectors and repo agencies just to name a few.

Introduction

This book contains my methods, tips, tricks and secrets to getting the information needed to get the job done, whether its process serving, repossessions, bill collector, reporter, realtor or law enforcement. It discusses approach, advanced skip trace methods and is devoted to examining all avenues that exist to locating people. The complete solution for the challenge of locating hard-to-find skips.

Skip tracing is a lighter term coined from "tracing a skipped debtor" or "tracing the debtor who skipped out." I've always thought it was a descriptive term for what an investigator does. If you have a nose for investigations, or you're just plain nosey, you may be in the right business.

I've worked as a skip tracer since a friend in investigations taught me the ropes. Together we worked for years as a successful duo in the entertaining world of hunting repossessions. Every repo case that I worked on became a classroom of example. I've now been working for myself since 2001, and I can't imagine doing anything else. The driving force behind each assignment isn't always the paycheck that follows, but the sheer satisfaction that I found someone; I figured it out, and got it done.

People will go to amazing lengths to hide a car from the lien holder. I've seen pickup trucks chained to trees and trailer houses. Cars locked in locked in garages and even buried under massive tree branches with garbage piled high on top in the back of someone's yard. I've seen that in hopeless times folks will take desperate measures. Regardless, we still have a job to do.

There isn't any wizardry in skip tracing. We don't use crystal balls to find people; of course, we wish it were that easy. And if that were the case, we wouldn't have such good job security. Experience in the industry is what new clients are looking for in a relationship with a skip tracer. When you get an assignment today, it should be first run tonight and then hopefully the invoice will go out tomorrow. This is the fact-finding service that banks, law firms and finance companies want and need to keep their wheels turning.

Investigative solutions to recovery agents are turning very tech savvy. With the car cameras (license plate recognition systems) and GPS locator units (in some states both methods are illegal), allows repo men to get more collateral picked up in less time saving a wealth of money on fuel. However, when we get a smart debtor who takes off the GPS, or it simply becomes nonfunctional and your vehicle isn't sitting pretty in the driveway it's time to take the gloves off and get into some really good skip tracing.

Dissecting the Skip

It's only about 60% of the skips that you'll successfully locate using a database regardless if you are using one that is free or paid (it's actually best to use several and not rely on just one). For the remaining percentage, most recovery agents classify as either a hard to find skip, or collateral that's lost to the four winds. When I get to the end of my skip tracing rope, I turn around and climb back up again.

Keeping in mind, people have to do things in order to live. Those things are creating traceable accounts and are mostly credit based. Utilities, insurance, pizza delivery and even traffic citations create solid leads to the person that you're searching for. If a person isn't doing them on their own then they're in someone else's name. I've found quite a few skips living with someone listed on their reference sheet. It could be a boyfriend, girlfriend or a family member that the debtor moved in with to get a chance to get back on their feet.

There is even a smaller chance that the debtor you are looking for is in jail or in the federal prison system. This would be a good explanation for a lack of activity or gaps of time in a database, credit report activity or utility connection inquiries. Searching the jails to see if your skip is incarcerated would be just one more thing on the to-do list for your skip trace efforts.

Simple profiling helps you determine which direction to look. An age range of a person helps you speculate if you should be looking for their mother or a spouse or paramour. Another explanation of gaps in activity is that someone else is living with the subject. The next step would be figuring out whom that "someone else" is.

A Good Start

Skip tracing professionals have become more of a secret society with hush-hush details of how the job really gets done. There was a day when I was happy to tell my clients how I located a debtor until I realized some things that I did were either so very simple or industry specific. Now if I'm asked the question I'll reply, "Ancient Chinese Secret" or "I don't give my secrets away, that's why you have me!" I think it's important to keep your methods of finding people close to your chest.

If you reveal too much about your ways of getting someone found then you could lose a client to the idea that they could find someone as effectively as you have with the information that you've passed along innocently. You deserve the bragging rights, but don't give away the secret recipe.

In this book, I'm going to give you many of the best internet links that provide the top-notch results for skip tracing. I've collected lists of skip trace programs (both fee based and free) that will help you get people found, served, arrested, and collateral recovered. Then I'm going to tell you how I find people that don't appear on a database search.

I'm also going to explain how I use these databases to get right through to the simple process that finds your skip. I'm going to teach you how to turn your cell phone into a trap line, how to find out if someone opened your email and very quickly get a new forwarding address for only fifty five cents.

I've learned things that skip trace seminars costing thousands of dollars would teach by searching common terms related to locating people. When I started to skip trace, I had a Palm Treo and would spend my leisure time searching the internet for new resources. I'd never bought any books but there were many online blogs by investigators sharing tantalizing details of the hunt and how they found someone.

Never give up, know that if one thing doesn't work something else will, and if you reach the end of "something else," just simply start over from the beginning. Creating your own checklists and things to look for helps you create your personalized method and stay on track.

Process servers, law enforcement, repossessions, collectors and private investigators are just a few professions that use skip tracing daily and are always looking for ways to utilize new technology. Social media and the growing internet are the greatest searches in a skip tracer's tool box. This book will take you through my favorite online searches that have assisted me most successfully, and a few that are not so successful, but also worth a try.

There are many job opportunities where good skip tracing skills will help further your career. Just about every business, at one time or another, has had a debt owed to them and will need a collection agency. If you're able to locate a disappearing debtor, make some phone calls and get money collected for your employer, you will have become a uniquely valuable asset to your company.

I work as a self-employed skip tracer for repossessions and other areas of collections. On the average, I've made enough money to support my database usage and cover other business expenses from working out of my office. All my fees are contingent on getting the debtor found, and the car picked up or the note paid. As with most collection agencies, I either charge a flat fee or a percentage of what the debtor pays.

You'll notice my experiences are from a repo company's point of view. However, all methods can be applied for any skip tracing situation. Working in repossessions is quite good job security and provides an excellent investigative experience. People that hide vehicles have been known to be the worst level of deliberate skips that I've ever encountered.

In Texas, working at least three years with a repossession agency gives you the apprentice time that you need to obtain your private investigator license. Several states in the U.S. don't require any special licensing or registration is voluntary. City, county and state regulations vary from one region to another. I only mention this because there are different databases that cater to different sectors of investigations and recovery.

In a sprawling and growing city like Houston, Texas having your own transportation is a necessity. While there's the element of fraud that I come across, most debtors are hardworking people that have leases and utilities in their name. This makes a good database well worth the money and effort to have.

For years I worked from home without having a commercially zoned office, until I discovered new databases that required a professional license or a special type of insurance. Since I wanted to work for the bigger population of business owners, I opened a collection agency.

As soon as I started cold calling finance companies, new work came flooding in. I was able to hire staff and close many cases daily. I accredit this to my staff's keen eye and excellent skip tracing style along with their professional manner. The insurance is affordable, and the access to fresh information was an enlightening experience, but I quickly learned that there are some databases that don't freely open accounts for collection agencies.

Those databases require membership in an organization such as the Association of Credit and Collectors, and errors and omissions insurance. I personally don't carry errors and omissions insurance (E & O) but the rates are high for new agencies, and I don't really need it as I rarely contact debtors directly and our office does not take payments. If you want to offer this service, you'll need a third party collector's bond, which, on the other hand, is a very affordable bond and is required to operate as a third party collection agency.

I also don't collect money on behalf of my clients. If the debtor wants to pay I make sure that the amount is directly verified by the lien holder, so there is no confusion over any new payments due or interest that I may be unaware of. This keeps me out of trouble for misquoting any amounts. I suggest telling an auto debtor to pay the person that has the title, unless you have made other arrangements with your client.

A third party debt collectors bond is for collecting money on behalf of your client. Every skip tracer's work situation is different. You may find that it works better for you to collect on behalf of your client and subtract your fees before you forward the payment to your client.

Basic Needs

If you don't have a private investigator's license then you must be skip tracing for collections, in which most states is allowed. I work in Texas and I can skip trace for the purpose of collections but in Florida you must have a private investigator's license to do skip tracing for collections. At the date this goes to print, Florida is the only state that requires an investigators license to skip trace for the purpose of collections and if you're in another state and work on collection accounts in Florida, you'll need to have a collection license in Florida. This situation isn't true of every single state in the U.S. It takes just a phone call to your state to find out what you need regarding licensing to skip trace.

When you get your assignments from your client there are some important documents you'll need. The information that you need is referred to as personal identifiers. Identifiers are the name, date of birth, last known address and social security number of the debtor, co-debtor or spouse and recognized as the pieces of information that helps you differentiate your skip from one database or source of information to another.

- Credit application
- References
- Payment history
- Vehicle information
- Proof of debt (pay history that shows past due)
- Driver's license copy (hopefully enlarged)*

A good credit application will give you information from the debtor at the time the credit purchase was made. If you are a process server or non-collection based investigator and you're skip tracing from scratch and you may not have this information, however, there are other ways to get what you need.

*There are many details of a driver's license that cannot be seen in a normal photocopy. When you enlarge the document, you will be able to see small numbers that wouldn't have any importance to an average person, but in the world of investigations would allow you to obtain a driver's history or other state and driver's license-related information.

- First, middle & last name Street address
- City, state zip
- Own or rent?
- Previous address
- Home phone Cell phone
- Date of birth
- Social security number
- Drivers license number and state of issuance
- Spouse's information if legally married
- Place of Employment (POE)
- Employer's phone number
- Supervisor's name

- Position held and if works out in the field, address of post
- In case of emergency notify

References are wonderful to work from and if your client isn't currently getting references, make sure to get them on track. It's also important to remember that friends sometimes move in with other friends and maybe you'll find someone who knows where the debtor hangs out and a routine schedule giving you the break you need.

If the debtor's spouse is not part of a contractual obligation, get that information anyway. When you debtor skips, the sole traceable contact could be the spouse, and it's very possible the only way you will know their name is through original credit application and reference paperwork. If you don't have that information you'd have to search for marriage records in every county that the skip lived in before he lived at the address that your client provided to you.

An easy way to find a skip is through a parent or other family member. My mom always knows where I'm living and how to get me on the phone right away, and she can certainly get a message to me within the next day or so, even if she doesn't admit to it.

The collection laws in the United States prohibit any collector from discussing debt with anyone other than the spouse over the phone unless written or recorded permission is given in advance. This could be an excellent suggestion for your client to obtain in writing at the time of the sale so you can legally call and ask for collateral to be returned from family members and references without legal consequences.

Other suggested waivers that would be good to have:

- Cell phone
- Text message
- Email contact (Would include social media messages and email addresses provided by the debtor or later found for the debtor.)

Since emails, text messages and cell phone calls could be received by anyone because the sender cannot confirm that the debtor is personally receiving those communications, it's potentially a violation of the FDCPA. This same law specifically says that it doesn't apply to process servers that are skip tracing to serve papers regardless if it's a lawsuit related to a debt or not.

I've had a client that required two of the references have a publicly listed land line in the phone book. The idea is that a person who would have a published land line at the time of sale would also have a published land line when the debtor skips out on them. Furthermore, these folks that have land line phones are most likely to be stable relatives.

They may not know exactly where your debtor is, but they can find them or get a message to them. If you find one of these previously listed references is no longer listed, checking property records may be the next step for you. All my aunt's and uncle's own their homes and when they move, they are not renting but buying a new house to move into.

Land line phones are becoming obsolete and can't compete with the free features of VoIP phone connections and most flat-fee cell phone packages such as Verizon, Boost and T-Mobile.

Cell phones are disposable, and you may find out the entire list of phone numbers on a reference sheet are disconnected or wrong when you get the assignment, but if the address is provided you can skip trace the reference from that address possibly getting a current phone number or new address to contact them.

I reinforce the importance of getting references' full addresses to my clients when I only see names and cell phone numbers. It's a big piece of information that could mean the loss of an entire car.

Sometimes, I've seen an application ask for the debtors "places of interest." If they are a night clubber, honky-tonker or make it to church every service, you'll find out here. A little club in Porter, Texas called Players has seen its share of repossessions. The little beer joint is long and has one-car-wide parking all the way across the front of the club making it very easy for a repo truck to back in, pin a vehicle and make it out of the parking lot before the debtor has a chance to get off the bar stool.

 I've also noticed that people go to church where family and life-long friends attend so it could be worth the extra effort of finding out where that is. On one occasion, I "Googled" a cell phone number of an older man who was supposed to be involved in a church. Simply running the phone number with dashes gave me several websites where the minister's phone number was listed as a contact for the church with the psychical address.

Sunday morning came and the repo man was ready. He drove through the parking lot and found his repo. The one element that was overlooked came in the form of parking lot security. As the repo truck pulled out of the church parking lot onto the main road, there was someone following him closely.

When both vehicles entered the highway - the security guard's car came up next to the repo truck and smashed into it trying to make the repo truck pull over. Major damage was done to both moving vehicles; the parking lot security guard went to jail for aggravated assault with a deadly weapon. A shocking end to what was expected to be an easy repo.

The pay history is required documentation if you are a collection agency using any one of three major credit bureaus for skip tracing. You may have to prove that you are skip tracing for the purpose of collecting a debt, and it's a useful tool when speaking to a debtor too. My tone is always different with someone who is only a few months behind in contrast to someone who is more than five months behind. The difference is the possibility that a person could get current on the account.

I treat my first few phone calls as gentle reminders to get past-due payments in and for debtors who are months or even years past due, I simply ask where the collateral can be picked up right away. If I get a response such as, "I just talked to those people," I then say, "You haven't made a payment in five months." After that there will likely be a pause by the debtor, and you can take this opportunity to make a deal.

It's a good idea to let your client know that if there's any other piece of paper in the file that could possibly turn into a lead, to please provide it for you. I don't need or like to see contracts. The print is usually very tiny and there is not much useful information on it. I feel that it's a waste of fax paper and ink. I can get the proof of a past due debt from the pay card or a print out of the pay history.

However, there could be a utility bill in someone else's name in the file or notes of attempts to contact the debtor by an employee. Some of my clients have even been known to write down the license plate of the car the debtor came in order to make payments, if it wasn't their collateral. Those are details that could really help a skip tracer go in the right direction.

Be Better Than Your Best Database

Most skip tracers get the free databases noted and check them often for new information. Some good resources are from your local and state government. I've found a few debtors in jail and I keep my eye on their release dates. If I can't find the collateral, and they are in jail, I'm pretty sure that they will be driving it after their release. Sometimes I have no option but to wait.

Other city and county public records to search:

- Traffic court
- Jail
- Appraisal district (property tax & ownership)
- Water (usually city or county owned but can be privatized)
- Voters registration
- Marriage license applications (even those that didn't marry)
- Civil court records (lawsuits, divorces & custody modifications)

Searches that consist of looking to see if someone is on parole or probation aren't usually on a public database but could found as part of a criminal history search. This person's status should be public information and obtainable through a Freedom of Information Act form submitted directly to the Adult Probation office.

Most of the time for, Texas parole or probationers, I don't have a problem with getting a confirmation of status over the phone. If the person I am looking for is also being sought by the state of Texas, the officer has been more forthcoming with information that they could help me help them.

The only piece of information that I've never been able to get over the phone is a date and time of a probation office visit. But the same wouldn't be true for a process server. Someone serving papers would be able to get this information because the law specifically says that anyone deliberately preventing process of service is in violation of the law. State employees don't have the option of breaking the law to protect probationers and if they do, I'm pretty sure their supervisors would like to know all about it.

Sex offender database, I don't think to check this often enough, but it's online and free. Criminal history searches are available in many places and one of them is PublicData. They don't have every single state, but your state may be there. If not, find out where and how you can locate if someone has been convicted of a crime in your state.

Civil court records show you past divorces, child custody and child support obligations and to whom those support payments are paid to. They can show judgments and liens that will give you someone different to speak to about your skip shining a new light on your investigation. You might get new information from an old source if you keep digging.

- Publicrecordcenter.com
- Publicdata.com
- Knowx.com

- Check for online sources for: State driver's license
- Motor vehicle records
- Voter's registration
- Traffic court dates
- Family court dates
- Property tax records (appraisal district)

A simple Google search sometimes will reveal criminal convictions with mug shots, criminal records, Facebook's pages, relatives listed on Mylife.com, or even a new job. I've seen schools, and large companies have websites with department head listings and employees listed with job site addresses and email addresses.

Google.com is especially wonderful for people with unique names but don't stop with just Google. Bing and bing.com/social are also getting specialized with social media searches because Google has begun to omit certain search results:

- Mylife.com

If you can find a web site to access for your state driver's license and motor vehicle database, it's going to be a good one to keep. The most efficient searches that I do on a motor vehicle database are looking to see if the debtor has bought a brand-new vehicle and if that new car has an unknown address.

Process servers: this is an especially helpful search to know what vehicle your subject could be driving with the possibility of a good address on the registration. To find out what kind of car you're looking for go to Carfax.com and run the VIN on the main page. To find out if a car has been reported stolen the National Insurance Crime Bureau has a free search.

- Carfax.com
- Autocheck.com
- NICB.ORG/THEFT_AND_FRAUD_AWARENESS/VIN CHECK/VINCHECK

I also look to see if the registration is current or expired and by how long. This gives you a picture of what may be going on with the auto. If there is current registration then it could be driven daily.

Ways to search identifiers through any database:

- Name and address
- Name and city Name only
- Last known address only (looking for others that lived with the debtor)

When you are looking up driver's license information hopefully you will be able to see the driver's license (or I.D. card number, sometimes suspended drivers will have both, so keep your eye out!) address history with dates of every change of address, duplicate obtained or renewal.

You may also have a selection to see all the other licensed drivers at that address. If not hopefully your database will let you search an address only without names so that you can see every person that has ever used that address. It's just another search that could yield associates of the debtor in your skip tracing efforts. In Texas we use:

- Datatraxtexas.com Nationwide Data Provider (Also found at new.datatraxonline.com)

I use the same search method for the motor vehicle database. Entering just the address to see who else has bought a car and registered it there, running name and city only to see if I can locate a new vehicle bought by the debtor at a fresh address and searching the name only statewide (or nationwide in other databases that will allow) to check for registrations out of the city when the debtor's last known address was.

Don't forget to run the VIN (vehicle identification number) alone through the database to see if the auto has been resold, re-registered or has a different notification only address on the title. Make notes of any new license plate numbers. If you're a process server or bounty hunter keeping tabs on license plate numbers greatly increase your success.

If you are looking at extremely expired registration, then the vehicle could be sitting in a garage or hidden away in someone's backyard. If you find yourself looking at a current registration, it's possible that there is good insurance for the vehicle which a little help from a friend in law enforcement could reveal a policy number and insurance company.

Carfax is an excellent resource that will tell you if the vehicle has been inspected at a state authorized inspection station. Of course, if the inspection is newer, you may find good auto insurance provided as well. How do you find out who the inspection station is? Call the state.

Voter's registration is a very reliable source of locating a new address or a family home address. The presidential election in 2008 that elected President Obama was a stirring of every soul in United States. The message was "Change," and it was clear America was ready for a huge change as many Americans registered to vote who had never voted in their entire lives.

From these new voters, hundreds of unknown addresses were gleaned. People who I had been searching for suddenly surrendered current address information. Why you may ask? Because if you intend on walking out of your front door to go to a voting booth; you are going to the one closest to your house.

Where I live in Harris County, Houston, Texas, there are several police departments that post online information regarding traffic court dates and even warrants. I'm able to search by name, driver's license or I.D. number and date of birth. Histories of court dates that are old and closed cases also may come up that include old drivers license addresses as well. Running those old addresses could give me new names of family members and associates who the debtor once lived with.

When someone gets a traffic ticket, it's possible that the address given for the ticket is a completely different address from the driver's license. This is the information that I'm looking for. This is my golden nugget.

You might stumble across an upcoming court date or hearing, which is good news if you are trying to get a subject served or a car repossessed.

- Warrant Toll Free Hotline 1-800-686-0570 –Texas

You may find that your subject has a warrant for his or her arrest, and you can use that as a bargaining chip for the surrender of a vehicle. Just use your imagination! This idea also goes for sex offenders. I've found several sex offenders that were not living at the address that was reported to the state.

This is a felony. I tell the sex offender that he has two hours to clean out the vehicle and give me an address where it can be picked up, or I'm going to file an affidavit with the sheriff's office, and he's going back to jail. This move never fails for probation and parole violators as well.

Profiling the Skip

Psychology is important to consider when beginning your skip tracing process. When begin to study paperwork and it's a young male, I instantly know that I need to find the mother. If it's an older woman-I may be looking for her paramour or grown children. If your debtor is not applying for credit and isn't doing the normal things people do when they move, then someone is doing it for them. The type of references and information on the credit application will lead you to gut level hunches in patterns of behavior that categorizes a skip.

Searching the address only, with no names, through a few of your databases may yield the best results if the debtor has already been living with the paramour or other family members. You will be able to tell who associates are because there will be a record of that person living at that address at the same time your debtor was.

Racial profiling comes into play on a less extreme level. In our big city it's very unlikely to see a black family living in a Hispanic neighborhood and vice versa. Birds of a feather really do flock together and in residential neighborhoods, if a mom or grandmother owns a home that is paid for - you should keep your eye on that house. If for no other reason, the skip may go to visit family and get a good meal.

I've seen for myself during the past and ongoing recession that grown children move back home when they can no longer afford to live on their own. It could be that the debtor is back in college, living at the parent's house due to no job, or the parent needing financial help from the child. Repossession chances are greater for the repo to be parked in the driveway or in the street since mom and dad are probably going to occupy the garage.

Some credit applications may ask for the names and ages of the debtor's children. You can't skip trace the children, but just knowing that the debtor has children helps you determine how far away the debtor moved. As a repo man or process server, you might be able to spot your skip waiting in the parent pick-up line at the old school or at another school in the same district.

During the school year the move may have been inside the child's area for the same school, mid semester the move could be to another school in the same school district or to a completely new area. Also if you find a new address close to the old address, most likely it's good because of the close move allows children to stay in the same school.

A mother always knows where their child is and more importantly, a daughter knows exactly how to get her mom on the phone right that second. I've spoken to many daughters that say they don't know where their mom is or even have a number to call her. Rest assured, just a few minutes after we disconnect, that mother is on the phone calling me asking exactly what it is that I want.

Databases

I don't rely on only one data provider. They all have strengths and weaknesses-gathering their information from different sources at different times. Sources of fresh information could be insurance applications, credit headers, magazine subscriptions or a retailer's customer database.

Nearly all the databases that can be obtained will let you search by address, social security number, and name in a variation of ways. If you get a P.O. Box as a fresh address, simply run the P.O. Box address alone in the databases to see who else is using the box. You may have some joyous results with some brand new people to skip trace.

Just make sure you check your dates as verification that the people are actually associated (lived at the address the same time your skip did). You may find a new record for an old box owner. Those new records from old occupants are likely to be collection accounts that are using the old address to pull new credit reports. Check and double-check your reports and compare them to find the common links.

Social security numbers can be a very annoying part of skip tracing. If you don't have one, sometimes it can be hard to get it. Especially if you don't have a database that allows you to see the entire social security number. There are a handful of databases that for extra verification of your business credentials and an on-site inspection, will grant you visibility of the full social security number.

It's obvious when people transpose numbers deliberately or use fake social security numbers thinking it will help them get a better deal. If you run the name and city only you will see all the people with that name, with distinctive dates of birth letting you know they are different people. If you study your report and go down the list you may spot the same person at the same address for a span of a few years using several different social security numbers.

And, of course, running only an address through the databases will show you every person that has ever lived there with dates of birth, social security numbers and dates of the record beginning first and possibly last reported. It's a common thing for a husband and wife's social security to be swapped with one another. I've had the idea this happens when property is jointly owned and the reports to the credit bureau have crossed over as the other spouse's number. I don't think this is intentionally fraudulent.

My very first database was Accurint. It's a good database but sadly is no longer offered to the home-based business (at the time this book goes to print), and collection agencies must carry E&O insurance to currently get a new account. Accurint is owned by the Lexis Nexis Corporation which owns many other databases such as IRBSearch.com and Knowx.com which the latter does have some free searches but focuses mainly on public records and property ownership records.

One of my favorite searches is on Accurint and done by entering a date of birth, a first name and a city. Even in Houston, a city of nearly four million people, I've been able to find my skip with this search.

- Accurint.com
- Irbsearch.com

- Knowx.com
- Merlindata.com

IRB is the version for law enforcement, private investigators and other professionally licensed businesses, and Accurint is more for collections skip tracing, small business and process servers. The pricing structure has greatly increased over the years and Lexis Nexis, having very fresh information, does adjust its fees accordingly.

When I began using it in 2001, most searches were only twenty-five cents. Accurint does offer good pricing plans now on the most-used searches but make sure your insurance is the right kind or the application process will turn into a frustrating event.

I use Findmyskip regularly. It's a favorite database that I still use with information pulled from many resources and compiled with excellent results. This is a pay-per-click database that updates often and has found new information on my hardest-to-find skips. If I've exhausted all efforts to find someone, I check this database about once every 7 to 10 days. New information could be scrubbed into the database on any given day from any source so it will pay off.

- Findmyskip.com

Because I'm a licensed and bonded collection agency I have subscriptions to both Experian and Equifax. These databases are really like getting the gossip straight from the horse's mouth. Of course, Transunion has their own skip trace database also.

Equifax has stronger information for the state of Texas (and most of the southern U.S.) and Experian is used by more multi-family communities, both have separate skip tracing databases that can be accessed without pulling credit or credit headers.

Equifax's skip trace database is called First Search and Experian's is called Collection Advantage. Both very affordable tools that will get your job done and get you paid. How the information is gathered is every skip tracers dream. At the very moment someone applies for a utility, residential lease, auto loan, credit card or mortgage, a credit application is completed and a full credit report (or just a score to determine deposit amount) is requested through an online portal.

When the information for the applicant is entered into the online form, it goes directly into the main brain of the credit bureaus and into a separate database for skip tracing. The reason why these separate and very important databases are so great is that someone must use the same address three or more times before it appears on the header of a credit report.

A new and different address, even only used just once, will go directly to the skip tracing database. This process takes only a few days to show after receiving the new information. Other databases such as Accurint, IRB, Tracersinfo and Mircobilt all buy information from these sources and could take many months for them to obtain. So, if you are able to get it directly from the big guys, you will save yourself time and money.

Another thing to remember when studying the dates and addresses on the credit bureaus is when you see an address that is an older address appearing with a new date, don't be alarmed. Continue to study the residential history because this can mean one of two things:

-A collection agency is pulling the credit report with old information, looking for new information.

-The skip has moved back to the previous address because it's a family member's home. Check ownership of the home to verify.

For employment searches Experian charges an extra fifty cents. You can get any reported place of employment information with Experian's Collection Advantage. Equifax divides their information into another database called The Work Source that provides the information on a no hit - no fee basis. So, if there is no hit, there is no registered job with The Work Source and there is no charge.

- Experian.com/esolutions
- Eport.equifax.com/eport/login.jsp
- Microbilt.com

Note: Equifax has a deposit so that if you have less than perfect credit, you may want to go ahead and choose to make the deposit for your account. If you are declined for an Equifax account on the basis of your credit you will have to wait six months to reapply and put up the deposit. You must be commercially zoned, have a road sign or sign on your door and have a listed business phone with 1411 information. The reason stated is so that a consumer may be able to locate you.

If you are a new business start up I want encourage you to give your collection agency a unique name. I've spent countless hours on the phone with consumers that insisted that I reported a collection account to their credit because I had a similar name to the agency that actually did report them.

Dirty little tricks skip tracers use...

If the skip moves close enough to the first address utilities may be transferred instead of applying for fresh connections. New accounts require new inquires to credit for the determination of a deposit amount. Furthermore, there are pre-paid utility services available for gas, electricity and water. These companies really assist someone in flying under the radar.

One utility that gets turned off and rarely paid is cable. I've found many skips because the old cable was disconnected and the debtor opted for a brand new Direct TV or Dish account.

One more new database that is showing muscle is Skipmax. For just a quarter you can get some jaw-dropping results. There are some manual searches that can be done for you, and the new bank searches are great for the judgment collectors looking for assets. This is the one to have and keep forever!

- Skipmax.com

If you have a larger scale business and can search in volume (batching) Core Logic has a great database for our times. It records new telephone, address and employment information from payday loans, rent-to-own, title loan and other lenders that inquire into thousands of consumer via teletrack.com. It has a few other products that would be attractive to asset searches and judgment collectors as well.

Ancestry.com has been a place where family goes to look for their roots. It also has a social security death index as part of a paid subscription. The confirmation that a debtor is deceased turns your investigation in another direction.

- Ancestry.com

At this point, you need to find out where the debtor lived when he died and look for any will filed with the probate court in the county where the deceased lived. Your search is going to be for the next of kin or executor of the estate. While Skipmax.com has a social security number validation search that costs fifteen cents, a free search for social security validation is:

- Ssnvalidator.com
- Masterfiles.com
- Publicdata.com - Not fresh data.
- Tracersinfo.com
- Ustracers.com

Need to break a P.O.Box? Just run the box information in the search field for the street name. For example, if there is one search field for address numbers only, leave that blank and place the entire address line in the street name field, and then the city and state in those appropriate search fields.

Don't use any names, leaving the name fields blank will return all individuals that have ever used that P.O. Box or address giving you dates to gauge your investigation with. This is one method to locate family members and even verify new residents of an address or a P.O. Box owner that is obviously unrelated to your skip.

If at any time you locate a new address for the debtor or a close family member, don't make contact with the debtor on the new phone number associated with the new address. When the debtor answers the phone and speaks to you they will instantly know that if you have their new phone number, you probably also have their new address and any collateral that was sitting in the driveway before your phone call, won't be sitting there anymore.

Free!

When pay databases don't work right away to locate your skip, turn to free databases and public records. These searches are the ones that I use to legally skip trace a reference or family members whom I believe would shed some light on my investigation.

- Civil court dates (Search the debtor as plaintiff and defendant)
- Family court filings (Divorce, child support enforcement or modification.)
- Property ownership (Tax records)
- Marriage license application
- Informal marriage registration (Marriage by proxy)
- Business name registration (D/B/A "doing business as".)

I don't recommend any pay database or people searches that market to the general public. Don't pay these outrageous fees to find your skips. These are not credit based searches and will not return results that you need to get your subject found. I've used them before and the data comparison showed me the information is old and obsolete. Free databases provide the same exact information. If there is ever a time when I use a paid public database I am reminded that I get what I pay for. Nothing new and nothing current.

If you are skip tracing with no credit application or other paperwork that would give you personal and unique identifiers, these free sites will give you (hopefully) some starting information. With a long and ever growing list of free and incredibly affordable sites - greatly improving the internet skip tracing process. I'll give you the ones that are most productive for me:

- Zabasearch.com
- Pipl.com
- Veromi.com
- Kgbpeople.com
- Spokeo.com

Zabasearch was the first online database compiling all kinds of public information (and maybe a few not so public) into a website accessible by the entire world, at no cost. When I think of skip tracing from scratch, I think of Zabasearch.

I can take a name and a city and usually come up with a narrowed down list of possibilities for the actual identity and then skip trace from there. I found my son's father in a tiny southern California town using Zabasearch. He had my son with him and they bother had been missing for more than 5 years. You never know what you may turn up in the free databases.

Pipl.com is also unique in a way that it searches every dark corner of the internet and pulls up hard-to-find Facebook, Myspace and other social media networking sites along with any web site that mentions your debtor's name.

I say, "hard-to-find", meaning that I've searched Facebook on the site directly and didn't find an account for the debtor and no other pay database gave me results. There have been times when I hit the search button a second time and received slightly different results.

Veromi.com has impressed me with comprehensive government record searches. I do believe there is a pay version but I've done searches under the tab for employment and found D/B/A's (doing business as) that the debtor had recently registered in another state.

Kgbpeople.com is also a web site and social media scrubber but its special because of the watch dog feature where the system emails you updates on the names you have flagged when there is new information. There is also an iPhone app making it very convenient.

Spokeo.com takes a different angle and implies that it has access to credit by offering to let you buy a package with a credit "temperature reading". While I've never used this feature because it would not really help me find a skip, the site is still a good resource to locate information when you have absolutely none to begin with.

Verification

Verifying new information you find is an extra step to save you or your field agent some gas. If it's a repossession-you don't want to make contact when you find a new address before its first run by a repo truck. If you do make contact, and the vehicle was sitting in the driveway, it won't be anymore. The same principal could be applied to any other reason for skip tracing.

The comfort zone of no contact with creditors is broken when you make that first phone call. If a debtor used a new phone number and a new address on a credit application and you've called the new number, the debtor will instantly know they have been found. Extra effort and sly trickery will have to be used to get the door open and collateral picked up.

Another favorite method of verification is sending a postcard in the mail. I use postcards that have simple messages such as, "I've been trying to contact you, please call me at 555-5555". If you truly don't want to rouse suspicion and you just want to know if the house is vacant and the mail is not forwarded you might try a postcard with an unassuming pretext such as a carpet cleaning advertisement or perhaps a, "We missed you at church" postcard.

I originally used postcards because of the reduced postage rate. Now postcard stamps are nearly as much as a first class letter. I preferred using postcards also because I can print them myself using Microsoft Publisher.

You can use Google Voice phone numbers for those types of devious pretexts where using your real cell or office number wouldn't be convenient or give you protection. Google Voice is free, although it's not currently a trap line. I did read about future plans to add this feature so keep your eye on it.

http://www.google.com/voice

The return address on your mail can give you current forwarding information and therefore making the first class stamp on the postcard (postcard stamps are first class) worth more. USPS.com gives you examples of the different ways to ask for information that will give you different results.

The most used format with the best results:

Valerie McGilvrey
P.O. Box 0000
Anytown, US 00000
ADDRESS SERVICE REQUESTED

If the mail forwarding on file has expired the postcard will come back with the forwarding address on a little yellow sticker that is placed over the debtor's address.

If the mail forwarding is still in effect, the mail piece is sent on to the debtor and a copy of the postcard's addressed side is imaged onto a bigger postcard with the new address printed just under the image of your mail piece and sent back to you directly from the United States Post Office.

This postcard is called a Form 3547 and when you get it, there will be an extra fifty five cent fee due. This is absolutely wonderful if your skip is not appearing in any other database searches and no neighbors who know to where your skip has moved to.

I keep dollar bills and quarters inside my mailbox so when I get the Form 3547 back I don't have to stand in line at the post office to get them. It takes anywhere from 7 to 21 days for this USPS postcard to be mailed to you.

The other terms used on outgoing mail are listed with explanation on the USPS.com site. Go here to read all about it:

- http://pe.usps.com/businessmail101/addressing/specialAddress.htm

When I'm trying to each out to a debtor and all I can do is reach out to the associates or family that I find using all my resources, I send mail, "In Care Of", to the debtor via all the family members that I've located.

Valerie McGilvrey
℅ Debra Smith 1000 Main St.
Anytown, Tx 00000

I've mailed thousands of letters and personal note cards in pretty colored envelopes addressed this way. Each with pretty and colorful postage stamps and colored ink to personalize the mail piece. The extra effort is to ensure my letter is opened. I don't want it to be mistaken for junk mail or a collection letter.

I surely will get a phone call from the associate that the % (in care of) is addressed to and most of the time that letter will get my debtor to call me, or provide me with more information to help along in the skip tracing process.

Making Contact

I've always thought that skip tracing followed the rules of marketing. You have to see it, read it and hear it about eight times before you consider using that product when the need arises. The process of getting information into the long-term memory could be compared with the process of continuing your efforts to reach out to a skipped debtor. It takes about three encounters for the brain to store information in long term memory. It could take that many attempts to contact your debtor through references and family members in order to grab their attention and return your phone call.

When I go through the references listed I call the family members first. Some other in house collectors may have already called the debtors friends so much that you are treated just like another attempt to collect a debt. A debtor's skeptical friend may pass along the messages, but not with the seriousness that a mother or father would.

Have you ever worked sales? Anything you have ever learned about selling and closing a deal would apply to making contact to collect a debt. Over the years I've seen books line the bookstore shelves with psychological tips and secretive tricks to entice a buyer to sign on the dotted line. Those same ideas and sales methods should be applied to skip tracing and collections.

I know having a rough day, too many cups of coffee and the normal routine of hang up calls can set anyone on edge, even a bill collector. Although you may think you have nerves of steel every once in awhile we all need to take a break. If nothing more, but to reset your mood and attitude. Checking your tone of speaking to make sure that the agitation of the lost progress on the previous debtor's phone call doesn't carry onto your next one.

Collection laws (FDCPA) prevent third party collectors from making harassing phone calls, threats of filing charges and jail time. Quoting the law is actually unlawful and could land you and your client in court. Don't assume that a debtor is not recording their own conversations at the instruction of an attorney. You won't have been the first collector to call them. These laws don't apply to process servers or the actual owner of the debt.

- Threaten to garnish wages where it's not lawful
- Don't contact the employer about the debt
- Threaten imprisonment or criminal punishment
- Report a financed vehicle as "stolen"
- Impersonate an attorney
- Impersonate law enforcement or any other government employee

The four states that don't allow wage garnishment for collection debts are Texas, Pennsylvania, North Carolina and South Carolina.

Another unique sales technique that works in conversation with debtors is called mirroring. Described as copying your debtor's speech patterns while reflecting accent and rhythm because we like and respond to people who are who are most like ourselves. This has turned out to be some pretty interesting social psychology. It could take some time to master but when you do it does increase results.

When you examine other sales techniques, envision howthey can be applied to your skip tracing process. With thousands of free blogs on the topic you should be able to develop your own personalized program and skip trace methods. How different is collections from sales? Your suave character dripping in kindness and willing to go the extra mile to make something good happen for a client and a debtor is very much like sales.

What do you say to references? I've a few suggestions for you and you may be able to create new questions that are not illegal to ask and are not giving away the debtors personal debt information. Of course, I'm extremely kind and polite when talking to a debtor's family. When someone answers the phone I always set peaceful a tone by saying, "Hi, how are you doing?"

After the greetings have been exchanged I will then say, "My name is Valerie, and I'm calling from XYZ Auto Sales. Is Joe Cool there?" I ask the person that answers the phone if they have something to write with, a pen and paper so that I can leave a message. This request is always met with a pause, and you will hear the person on the other end of the phone rustle for something to take your message on. I've noted in the past that if I don't ask this directly my message won't get written down and possibly forgotten.

Sometimes the debtor is actually available, so be prepared to make a very polite demand for the collateral. I get the very best results by saying, "Hi, this is Valerie from XYZ Auto Sales. We need an address to pick up our 2002 Nissan Exterra." Sometimes you will get an address, and sometimes you will get hung up on. If a debtor has something to say, it will be at this moment. I've heard all kinds of excuses such as:

- ✓ I paid that already
- ✓ It's been repossessed already
- ✓ I gave it to my cousin (Or someone else) and good luck finding it.
- ✓ It's in the shop (Please give me shop name and address) and I don't remember where that shop is.
- ✓ It was stolen and wrecked (Call the police department to verify and continue with asking for insurance contact and claim numbers.)

If the debtor has already paid the note, you can ask for those details. You probably already have the pay history in front of you and will be able to specifically quote the last pay date, the past due amount, late fees, and collection fees. I've had plenty of debtors tell me that a car note was just paid and they were referring to a small payment made over 30 days ago. Hopefully you will get more information on how to get the collateral back or the debtor's commitment to pay on a certain date.

Just think of all the conversations in which you asked someone an important question, and you got an honest answer. Remember that calm tone? Can you think of a time where you've had an argument (or maybe simple conversation) where you know who you knew was lying to you and the liar wouldn't admit it? In my experience I would say that the question becomes an argument as a defense to the lie.

A subject that overreacts, and screams at me (usually interrupting me multiple times) saying things like, "Your talking to the wrong person!", or, "I don't have it, I told you already." Protesting in atone and insistence that are used in an attempt to convince me to give up completely. It never fails that someone who continues to protest and behave unruly does absolutely know where our collateral is, and most of the time they are actually driving it themselves.

Lies work a bit into our attitude, tone of voice, and the language (body language too) we use to skate around the truth. Worried about being caught on the spot and feeling guilty. Therefore, are being stressed, touchy and dramatic. You can catch recognizing speech that is in a high pitch tone and hesitation to continue the conversation. The liar may even slip up and use a wrong work in their sentence because the brain is working hard to create the perfect "lie scenario".

Has anyone ever told you their car broke down and they left it on the side of the road? I'm pretty sure I hear this at least once a week. When I begin to inquire as to when and where the car is now, the debtor usually seems to draw a blank and can't remember any details. Answers to my questions draw vague descriptions of how the breakdown happened.

An honest mistake can happen with a debtor actually paying their car note up to date and the lien holder forgot to let you know. I make it a common practice to call the lien holder to verify that the debtor is giving me true or false information. It could also be that the debtor did pay some money on their balance, but the collateral stays in repo status until the note is all the way caught up.

What field agents do to verify your address:

- Talk to the neighbors
- Look to see if the light meter is running

Take the trash to look for information such as bank account statements or banking related papers, job information, return addresses on envelopes, or other items that would lead you to your goal.

Leave a card or note on the door asking for a return call (Use Trapcall.com). Look for the mailman delivering mail at the address.

Garbage gets you some quick and easy information. I was hunting a woman named Julia, and she was living in a house that was listed for sale. I drove to her home and knocked the door on several occasions and there was no answer. One day I noticed that the door bell which was usually lit was no longer glowing. A neighbor walking his dog came up to me on the front porch and told me that she was out of town and that when she is in town her, two huge black Labradors will be in the window looking out and barking at anyone in eyesight.

I worked on other things and a week later I decided to drive by and check to see if I see any dogs and yes, they were inside the house barking when I shut my car door. Her garbage was out on the street. I knocked on the door and got no answer, so I popped my trunk open with my remote and threw the two big bags of garbage into my trunk.

I'm never prepared to do garbagology, I normally pass on the trash, especially in the daylight but Julia was ignoring all attempts to make contact with her. She knew why I was knocking, and she just wasn't going to face me.

I drove over to a CVS Pharmacy and bought gloves and Lysol and got after my garbage search. I was indeed right when I noticed that the door bell button was no longer lit. One garbage bag was full of rotten food from her powerless refrigerator. This bag was from her kitchen and dining room area and had almost no paper in it except for some old grocery receipts.

The second bag was stacked full of papers. Invoices and work orders that came from Home Depot and Lowes for installation of appliances purchased by their customers. So, this was her big secret. She actually had two vehicles out for repossession with my client. One was a Ford F250 with a Tommy Gate, and the other was a Land Rover.

I had to find a repo company that would give me two or three repo trucks on this deal. I had a plan, and it worked. I called her and told her that my house burned down, and I've an insurance check for my appliances and five kids at home. I needed to get my appliances delivered and installed tomorrow with the promise that I had cash in hand for payment at the time of service.

She met me at Home Depot in her Land Rover, and the Ford F250 pickup pulled up right behind her. And three repo trucks swooped in and blocked both vehicles from leaving. Yes, it was a showdown, and yes. We got our cars.

Professional Licensing

In every state there is a department of licensing. I called the state and asked if I could get a list of professions that required a license and how I could get license information. Now the information is all online. Cosmetologists (hairdressers), electricians, plumbers, tow truck drivers, security officers and many other vocations require a state license to be obtained and maintained.

Insurance agents and claims adjusters are separately governed by the department of insurance as well as a few other jobs that require continuing education credits to be earned yearly. Security officers are registered and regulated by state government as well.

Searching the license information can take only a second of your time and most likely won't appear on any web searches done on Google.com or any other search engines. So, when you locate your state's licensing department bookmark it and run all your skips through it ever so often.

In Texas, we have several different resources for different types of licenses. The Department of Insurance governs insurance sales and adjuster licenses. The Department of Private Security has records for private investigators, alarm installers and security guards. The Texas Supreme Court website has the list of authorized process servers that covers the entire state of Texas.

Medical professions such as doctors and nurses (licensed positions only) are found in our state's Health Department records. I've found nurses and their job location at the very least and the human resources office for that medical center would have to supply the remaining information upon documentation. For example, serving papers.

A not so professional license to look out for is a hunting and fishing license.

Place of Employment

There are many reasons why you need to locate a place of employment on a skip. Also referred to as POE. For me, it would be to repossess their car for my client. For a mother, it would be for a wage garnishment on child support. For a process server, it would be for serving papers.

For those of us working on the collections side, we are working from a credit application and may have other resources to locate and confirm an old or a new job.

If the credit grantor had the debtor complete and sign an employment verification form, then this form would be good at a later date and can be used to verify a new lead employment.

Here is the rundown of my process for locating a POE: Run all the database pulls and print them.

Look for phone numbers that are newer or different than what you have for the skip and Google them to see if they are connected to a business of any type.

- 411.com does a great job of reversing business phone numbers and addresses.

Check out the Google Street View and see what type of building is at any address that you have found. Sometimes small businesses use mail drops boxes such as a UPS Shipping Center. This is not necessarily a dead end, but just a bump in the road.

When pulling a credit report remember that a debtor has to use the new address or job three or more times before it will appear on the credit header. So, if you are getting old job information, wait awhile and pull it again.

Running license plates in the driveway may give you a commercial vehicle. That would be the likely employer of your debtor. Also, neighbors may be able to answer a direct question like, "Do you know where he works?"

Military Personnel

I've been stumped in the past when I couldn't find someone that has enlisted. I've not discovered a better sure fire solution other than calling a recruiting station and asking the officers there to do a computer search. If you let them know you are serving papers you will get full cooperation.

Marine Corps written requests (does not forward mail): Commandant of the Marine Corps

Headquarters, USMC

Code MMSB-10

2008 Elliot Rd – Rm. 201

Quantico, VA 22134-5030

Telephone requests: 1-703-640-3942

Retired from Marine Corps: HQ U.S. Marine Corps

Manpower & Reserve Affairs (MMSR-6) 3280 Russell Road

Quantico, VA 22134-5103

Air Force will forward one letter per each request.

Active Duty, Retired and Reserve:

U.S. Air Force – World Wide Locator AFPC-MISMDL

550 C. Street West

Randolph AFB, TX 78150-4752

The Army locator will provide current addresses for active duty individuals: World Wide Locater

U.S. Army Enlisted Records

8899 E. 56th Street Indianapolis, IN 46249-5301

Coast Guard will provide current ship or station and phone number of active duty:

Commandant (CGPC-ADM-3)

U.S. Coast Guard 2100 Second St. S. W.

Washington, DC 20593-0001

Navy

Navy World Wide Locator
Naval Personnel Command
Pers-312
5720 Integrity Drive
Millington, TN 38055-3120

Bankruptcy

When someone files bankruptcy they have complete debt protection. You can no longer make contact with the debtor for collections or repossessions. The information that they used to get their bankruptcy case filed is public information. You can get it by calling any Federal Bankruptcy court and point blank asking for it.

It's always a good practice to get the information and make notes of the job reported and address and phone info along with any upcoming confirmation dates that would be helpful to you. You can also get a free online account and view documents recorded and future court dates and to get the toll free number in your district.

Past bankruptcy filings will also be on the court's computers and you may receive that information as well.

- Pacer.gov
- Pacer.gov/phone_access.html

Social Media

Social media – dive right in – currently there are no federal restrictions on contacting a person on social media but if you don't send collection messages via Facebook you will have a better chance of gleaning info that will help you in the long run.

Honestly, Facebook has been a resource that has allowed me to get in touch with the most difficult skips. I understand each company may have its own social media standards for making contact on Facebook and other sites like it. Facebook has some of its own standards as well. There are keywords that are flagged when you send a message to someone and the recipient can report your message as harassment. Facebook has started charging $1.00 to send an email to non-friend. The new standard is now messages from unconnected people and business go into a separate folder.

Plucking out a skips Facebook email address is quite easy with the URL formula. Take my Facebook for instance, the URL is:

https://www.facebook.com/vmcgilvrey?fref=ts

The words between the / and the ? is my Facebook.com email.

vmcgilvrey@facebook.com

Creating an account that relates to the debtors circle of friends is an effective method. If you can see the debtors daily comments you may be able to narrow your search down and in some cases get an exact location of where the debtor will be and at what time.

I don't know who is using Facebook as a skip tracing tool, but I'm still surprised at the amount of information that you can find on Facebook these days. In a world where privacy is constantly in the news you would think more people would have their accounts private and list of friends completely blocked from outsiders view.

Update on Facebook profiles. Forbes reported that Facebook no longer allows profiles to be hidden from searches either on the site itself or web based searches such as Google.com, Bing.com/social or Yahoo.com.

Posts made will sometimes offer a location via smart phone. You will see location information under the post itself and it will start with the word near. Some Facebook users have location sharing turned completely off for random posting from their cell phone.

It's a nice day when I look for someone on Facebook and find that they have a completely public wall or make public postings. Those people feel most comfortable with what they are doing and the level of information that is being posted. Hopefully it's enough to let you know what direction you should go in.

If you can be "friends", you can get email addresses from the "about" section, phone number and maybe new job information. The possibilities are limitless now that we have moved from a "I did this" and into a "I'm doing this right now" society.

People will tag one another for events such as church and family gatherings, invitation to events, going out for ice cream or anything that they deem important for all their close friends to know. Denial of friendship on Facebook is a bummer for me. The only thing that I can do to hopefully have a future "friendship" is to make a connection with another person on the friend list.

Did you know that you can reverse a cell phone number on Facebook? Just enter the phone number where you would a users name and if that phone number is associated with an account, those accounts will appear in a list.

Then there will be a "mutual friend" and a comfort zone will have been created. I've had a few debtors that send messages back asking who I'm and how I know them. The easiest way to get around a direct question is to not answer it.

Photos are another great source of information. I've seen many people posed in front of a new car with a license plate that I could run and get a new name and address. It may be a friend's house or family but it's something that I didn't have before. Study images and look at the surroundings.

Scan pictures for unique things that you may be able to spot in person such as a window on the front door with burglar bars or a business sign in the background. Street numbers on the front of houses or curbs are worth noting.

You may be able to match a street number to a street name in a later database search and then you'll know you have a live address. When you see pictures taken indoors literally look at the window area of the picture to see if you can see anything like cars in the driveway, plants or neighbors houses.

If you are able to find photo's on any other part of the internet, meta tag information could be obtained free from the picture. There are several different software packages, most free, on the internet to download that use the process of copying the photo into the software for latitude and longitude information. Facebook strips this information from pictures. One resource is:

- Photome.de/home_en.html

It really gives you a chance to solve one piece of the mystery by putting together an employment history and current status. LinkedIn also connects with Twitter so if the user has a Twitter account you'll be able to find that account also.

Blogging is not a thing of the past although I think that Facebook connections and updates have taken up a huge need for self expression and communicating with family that lives far away.

A Google search should reveal a blog anywhere on the internet and if you don't see anything for your debtor on the first page of the search results - continue onto the next screens of the search results. It's worth the extra few seconds to scan the additional pages, because you never know what you will find if you just keep going.

- Boardreader.com

Although I use the name Google regarding search engines, there are others that can be used. A good one that I re-discovered is Infospace.com. Altavista.com is another one that I've used since the first day surfing the internet and Webcrawler.com is yet another for the list.

I had a very frustrating skip that several repo companies had before me. This girl was a first payment default, and she had an extra reward on her car as well. I sat down one evening looking over the paperwork searching over every line looking for that one little tiny detail that could lead me to her or someone who was close to her. I took all of the reference names and Googled them.

Dirty little tricks skip tracers use...

The Grandmother passed away, and her obituary was in the local newspaper and listed in the Google search. My debtor was listed as a survivor in the obituary and the funeral was three days away. I was pretty excited to hear that the car we were looking of was sitting in the parking lot of the funeral home, and it was picked up with no problems.

- Altavista.com
- Infospace.com
- Webcrawler.com
- LinkedIn.com

LinkedIn has possibilities for locating hard to find skips. If your skip is on a professional level the chances are greater for getting good information from this site that markets to professionals making new contacts to enrich their business or find a new job. The nice thing about LinkedIn is that you cannot block someone, the only way to get away from someone is to remove the connection.

If you are using an upgraded paid subscription you will be allowed to view full profiles and scan them for any new information. You can see groups that one belongs to and go forward with a well devised pretext to make contact and connect.

Email

I've seen quite a few credit applications request email information. I don't spend a lot of time sending email to debtors and I don't think many of my emails have ever been returned. I've been concerned that my email could be misconstrued and taken out of context.

When you are sending email the debtor can't hear the tone in your voice and you certainly can't hear the tone in theirs. However, if this is all you have, I say give it your best shot.

If you can get a reply from an email the email header could provide some useful information to an investigator that knows how to trace email. The trace provides an IP address and internet connection (ISP) for the computer that sent the email which in turn could provide an address upon subpoena.

To get header information from an email in:

Yahoo - scroll to the bottom of the email and you will see several different options in a row. The tab with an icon of a little gear is near the right-bottom side of the email. When you hover over it with your mouse it will say "More actions for selected emails". Click on this option and you will see "View Full Header". When this option is clicked on a pop-up window will appear with the full header information from the sender.

Gmail, Outlook, Hotmail, and AOL all have similar processes and you can learn the process by contacting the email provider that you use.

It's pretty easy to trace an email back to its geographic location; it's quite another story getting the information of the "Sender. You've won the battle learning the geographic location, but you haven't won the war. Interesting links to check out:

- Whatismyipaddress.com
- Spamcop.net

When you are ready to send email and you don't want to use your own email address or want to send an email from a corporate email address; there are many options to choose from. These two email spoofing sites are free:

- Guerrillamail.com
- Emkei.cz

Not getting a reply at all from sent emails is what usually happens to me. It's so easy to avoid reality by not even opening the email and just immediately sending it to the trash. I remember when I got my very first email account from AOL. An awesome feature of AOL was a notification from AOL letting me know that my email was opened. Today we have those options with these free sites:

- Spypig.com (Where did they get this name from?)
- Didtheyreadit.com (free trial with paid subscription)
- Readnotify.com

The Phone

The phones you use in your office, your home office and your cell phone are the lifeline to skip tracing. I don't use my office phones to contact debtors so when my desk phone rings I know it's a client calling.

I've several Magic Jack VoIP phones that have saved me thousands of dollars on phone bills. Magic Jack, as well as other VoIP connections have call-forwarding, voicemail and caller ID. I'm a former Vonage customer and the service is exactly the same. Only Magicjack is the affordable and simplified version.

Currently there is no caller ID blocking for outgoing phone calls so if you are using Magic Jack to make collection calls you will receive incoming calls while you are on the phone. One way around that is make phone calls from your Google Voice account or use your toll free Ureach number to make outgoing phone calls.

This method keeps you in line with the Truth in Caller ID Act of 2006 by showing a real number that is your phone number that you can receive return phone calls and messages.

Google Voice is an outstanding free phone service that has oodles of features and is great for working from home. Only one phone number per email account is allowed however, you are not restricted to having a Gmail account to use the service.

You can sign up with any email. There is no IP restriction either so you can have multiple accounts with multiple emails.

- Magicjack.com
- Google.com/voice

Call spoofing is not a new technology and there are resources for the spoof calling service all over the internet. Using call spoofing allows any phone number to appear on caller ID that you designate.

The service calls you first, and then the phone starts ringing to the target phone. You will see the phone number appear on the screen that you program for that call. If you see "unavailable" then your phone number was entered incorrectly.

The big News of the World scandal revealed that Rupert Murdoch's employees of the tabloids used spoofing to secretively listen to voicemail messages and get information stored in the voicemails.

How that was done is the target phone didn't have voicemail password prompt turned on. This allowed the person that had the phone in had to call voicemail and listen to messages without entering a password.

When spoofing was used to call the target phone; the cell phone number and the caller ID number used were exactly the same. Some phone carriers have handsets programmed to call the cell phone number to listen to voicemail messages.

When the phone call came in it was routed directly to voicemail because the carriers network took it as the phone calling to listen to voicemail. I've seen spoofing used for standard pretext calls.

- Itellas.com

I've used spoof calling and pre-texting to get debtors set up for the repo agent. A very difficult account in Houston was assigned to me. The debtor's name was Fred and he drove a black Mustang with custom paint and rims. Fred owned a barber shop on the north side of Houston and he parked the car right in front of the back door of the strip center where his barber shop was located. I was told that he kept the back door wide open and he was close to the car at all times. The goal was to get Fred away from the car long enough for the repo truck to grab it and make a clear get-away.

I first looked for the landlord of the strip center. I was having trouble finding a land line phone number for the barber shop. I was thinking that there wasn't one and the land lord would have Fred's cell phone number. The first business that I called in the strip center was a realtor. A very nice lady answered the phone and I asked her if she had any information on the barbershop and she said, "Yes, it's for sale!"

Sometimes you don't need to create a pretext, the opportunity just simply creates itself. When I spoke with Fred the first time I told him that the realtor in his strip center gave me his number and told me his barber shop was for sale. He immediately started telling me all about his shop. I told him it wasn't for me, but for my little sister and we all needed to meet and look at the store.

He invited me to lunch the next day, I named a place close to his barber shop that didn't have any windows in the front of the restaurant and two sets of huge wooden doors to go through. This way he would park, go inside and wait for me and not be able to see his Mustang getting towed away. Fred showed up right on time and sat in his car waiting for me. After a while he got out, opened his truck and grabbed a towel and stated to shine his rims.

When the repo man called me and told me that Fred wasn't going inside I knew I had to call him. Fred answered the phone and I asked him to order me a hamburger. I told him I was about 8 minutes away and that I was starving to death. He told me he was waiting for me in the parking lot. I said, "Oh no! Don't wait for me outside; it's over 100 degrees right now!"

After he got off the phone with me he very slowly got out of his car and walked into the restaurant. Going through two sets of heavy wooden doors, with no windows, to get into the restaurant area. This gave the repo truck his 60 seconds to hook the Mustang and be down the road. Fred never called me again.

How do you feel about toll free numbers calling you? I don't answer them either. If I called debtors from a toll free number I would rarely get an answer because I think they are either a sales call or a collection call. Truth in Caller ID Act of 2006 has made it illegal to use deception (or call anonymous) on caller ID. This is why I've a cell phone to call debtors, especially for repossession debtors. Local phone lines get calls answered and messages returned.

When I make contact with debtors I enter the phone number in the contact list. It's an easy way to have all the debtors' phone numbers in one place. I also feel that people will call back a number that is recognized as a cell phone thinking it's possibly an old friend.

I send a postcard to every debtor that I don't have a good phone number on. I'm in search of USPS forwarding information on file as well as a note on the postcard asking to please call me. Quite a few of the phone calls I receive from the post card mailers have their caller ID restricted. I hunted for ways to overcome this because I know I can get an address from a phone number and I needed that information.

Please note that mailing postcards with debt Information is a violation of the law!

I discovered Ureach.com. Ureach provides a call announcing service to its customers that actually acts as a fail proof trap line when forwarded to another phone. I once had a desk phone forwarded to Ureach and then Ureach forwarded to my cell phone. It sometimes takes a few minutes for the blocked number to be unblocked and appear in the call log.

The number you get is toll free, receives faxes and gives you an email address.

- Ureach.com

Just a few years ago an amazing trap line service was made available called Trapcall. This is a service for cell phones only and works with the major networks ATT, Verizon, Sprint and T- Mobile (there is a feature to check your phone carrier on the site).

Once your cell phone is programmed any incoming phone call that you ignore is forwarded to Trapcall, reversed and sent back to your phone. A text message is then sent to your phone with the phone number; date, time of call and any name and or address information obtained.

Your account on the Trapcall website is feature rich with the ability to block certain phone numbers, make notes, nickname phone numbers and see a separate list of unblocked numbers. It also covertly records incoming phone calls.

The very first phone call I received after installing Trapcall on my cell phone was a restricted number. I immediately "ignored" the phone number (by pressing the hang-up button either once or twice-test your cell to learn this process), and the call was forwarded to Trapcall then sent back to my phone unblocked. I got a good address and the repossession was picked up that night.

- Trapcall.com – my personal favorite to use with pre-texting and mailing requests for a return phone call.

Just about all the databases have good phone reversal searches. A list of how I search phone numbers for owner and address information:

- Google.com - to see if the phone number is used in any online advertising, listed and published with a phone company, listed in a Craigslist ad or resume listed online.
- Whitepages.com - also a smart phone app. Charges less than $3.00 for monthly unlimited usage to reverse cell and landline numbers.
- Tnid.us - a free service that gives the caller ID information for a phone number.
- Stumpthemonkey.com –gives me about the same results as Skipmax. Skipmax.com

- Fonefinder.net This site has been up for many years and very trustworthy. Fonefinder is free, and I've even spotted a police investigator using it on a desktop computer on a true-crime show. This site will give you the name of the provider for the phone number and will let you know if you have a cell phone or a land line. Theres also has a link to click through to the carriers website.

If you run your phone number through all these resources you will know who the carrier is, and possibly get at least a zip+4 code on the phone record. Zip+4 codes narrow an address down to a section of about ten addresses on one side of the street. This really puts you in the zone.

The next free database to use is Melissadata. The search for getting an address from zip+4 is the one you need. This site has many free features that will keep you buzzing for a while.

- Melissadata.com

Sometimes, all that I can find on someone is a cell phone number. While collection laws are disapproving of calling a debtor on a cell phone, of course, there are many other ways to get information from it. New laws late into 2012 have made allowances for a debt collector to call a cell phone and also use text messaging service. The blog on Microbilt.com has information about all the changes to debt collection laws.

Our society has evolved into a digital world that is constantly on the move. Having a landline phone is not only a waste of money, in these times it's more of an inconvenience. Talk, text and web offered in unlimited package deals with really nicely designed phones have dazzled even the least tech-savvy individual.

Everyone now wants to have a cell phone that can give you access to a to a phone line, text messaging, email, Facebook, a camera and most now have a video camera anywhere you can go in one neat little package. One little device now replaces over a thousand dollars worth of electronics.

It's not legal to obtain detailed cell phone records by any means. This is not something that would do a world of good to have anyway. The outgoing calls that appear on a detailed bill are mostly to other cell phones and that would be a very time consuming and expensive ordeal to reverse them.

It's not illegal to ask for them to be provided to you if you want the records as a skip tracing tool for the future. In a situation where you are asking the potential debtor in order to gather documentation along with copies of the light bill, bank statements, insurance information and other required pieces of information on your list that you need to consider credit worthiness.

A fax line is a phone too. If its caller ID is blocked it would be quite unusual. If you have communication with your debtor a way you may discover his whereabouts would be to initiate a fax transmission to and from the debtor in a rushed period of time. For instance, if you send an agreement to the debtor for a quick payment plan that will get their car out of repossession and they must sign it and fax it back within that hour, you could get a fax number to where your debtor is going to be waiting for your fax and sending it back to you.

Most of the time this fax number is a mail store such as UPS or a grocery store and the fax number will be listed with all the search engines and on the web site of the store making discovering it's owner simplified.

Cease & Desist

Under Section 805(c) of the Fair Debt Collection Practices Act, a debtor can request in writing to a third party collector to cease and desist from calling or knocking on the door regarding the debt. This regulation does not apply to creditors directly. According to section 803(6), the FDCPA is specifically for those who attempt to collect "Debts owed or due or asserted to be owed or due another."

Therefore, a creditor (lien holder) collecting on debts owed to it-self is not considered a debt collector under the FDPCA and is not bound by its contents. In short, if you own the debt you can continue to make contact in person or by phone. If you are a third party collector or agent (repossession or recovery) of the lien holder, then you must stop all contact.

If you are not able to talk to your debtor at a reasonable time, then you may be able to lawfully call or knock the door at a later time than the law allows. Keeping good notes of all your other failed attempts, and that you are left with no choice but to make contact at a later or earlier hour.

Seasonal Skipping

When the summer begins I get a flood of requests for skip tracing from process servers and attorneys. Collection agency skip tracers have many more options than process servers can get their hands on.

The summer skips are mostly custodial parents that have moved and the non-custodial parent has filed to get their summer visitation enforced and perhaps their regular visitation simply restarted.

These are very expensive filings that are worthless if they can't be found to be served. Similar to people with open warrants for their arrest, custodial (or non) parents that are hiding could be secretly getting help from sympathetic family members. Skip tracing is more like a game for information to appear on the databases to work from. Someone hiding from child support obligations can be just as challenging.

People need things in order to live. Work, clothing, food, transportation, a driver's license, insurance, schools, doctors, electricity, etc... If someone disappears today, their current living situation would quickly expire and one of those necessities would have to be provided. If not obtained on their own, those would be expenses covered or provided by someone else. And eventually, all good things must come to an end.

Also, by the time when the skip starts doing things that will leave a footprint the databases will have updated with the new information. This is why I say, when one thing doesn't work something else will and when you get to the end, start over from the beginning.

From the debtor's point of view, the school year has ended and it's easier on the child to make a major move to another neighborhood or even a new city. Another time of year that is also popular for parents not allowing visitation and debtors making a major move is the end of the first school semester which usually is the beginning of Thanksgiving or Christmas vacation time.

Here is a list of databases that I don't use, but are good to know about:

- Infousa.com
- Denspri.com- Has driver's license photographs for some states.
- Iso.com- For the insurance industry and is a database of all insurance claims.
- Insightcollect.com
- Charitynavigator.com
- Degreechk.com
- Studentclearinghouse.org

What do background searches consist of?

Sometimes in skip tracing you need to do a background to get to the present. Some investigative jobs do background searches for potential employers. Here is a list of things that a background search may consist of. Any particular one of these things could be illegal in your state for the purpose of employment, but be necessary for approval as a tenant. This is another area that you must know your local statutes in order to do the job.

- Driving records
- Vehicle registration
- Credit records
- Criminal records
- Social Security number verification
- Education records
- Court records
- Workers' compensation – YES this is a public record!!
- Bankruptcy
- Character references Neighbor interviews
- Medical records – with signed release
- Property ownership
- Military records

- State licensing records
- Drug test records
- Past employers
- Personal references
- Incarceration records
- Sex offender lists

Only if those pieces of information are legal to obtain in your state or county for the purpose of employment screening. For example, California may not look at your credit report in review to determine eligibility for employment. However, this list does give a good idea of things that you can find out about a person's background that can bring you to the foreground.

The Ultimate Skip Trace List

Long ago when I started to skip trace, I made myself lists of things to do. Not because I would forget to look for someone in a specific search (ok, yes I've forgotten that there were certain things that I could do), but because it helped me discover new ways available providing information about my skip. I found my old list that I've shared before and there are a few things that I'm sure you already have on your list too.

My list became so very important to me, and it didn't take me long to learn that while I was searching for a skip in so many different directions, my skip was out there living life and eventually would leave a trail of bread crumbs for me to pick up on. This is why I say if one thing doesn't work, something else will. When you get to the end of your list, start all over again from the beginning of your list.

- Run social through all your databases and assimilate info.
- Run address only with no names to see who else would be living with your skip.
- Skip trace references for new addresses (yes I've had skips move in with family listed as references, and the family has a new address).
- If you discover a new phone number for the skip, work the phone number to bust it. You may discover a new address from the phone and not have to make your chase known.

- Voters registration. I'm pretty sure that people register to vote close to home. I've almost never seen voters registration address listed as a mail drop or post office box.
- My mamma told me that con men drive fancy cars. Check the DMV to see if there has been another vehicle purchased by the skip. My Texas database lets me run addresses only so that I can see who else has bought cars at the skips previous addresses. If the registration dates are in the time zone when I know my skip lived there, then I've discovered an associate and have a new direction to go.
- Marriage. When a skip totally disappears and has no inquires on any credit reports I think they are either in jail or dead. But sometimes they just got married and now have all the necessities of life in their new spouse's name. You may also find applications for marriage licenses that weren't turned in to the court house. Could be a wedding date was postponed or cancelled altogether.
- Look for civil lawsuits. People that have sued your skip love to talk. They want to find your skip too so that they can get a judgment paid.
- Yes, con men drive nice cars, and they usually have several D/B/A's registered in their name. Another great online search with your local state or county government. A reliable source for a nationwide search for those D/B/A's is Veromi.com
- It never hurts to ask the old apartment management office for the address where the deposit check was mailed to, if they skipped out on rent you may be able to get the "in case of emergency" contact and find out who else lived in the apartment and what other vehicles were listed on the lease.

- Send mail. ADDRESS SERVICE REQUESTED should be printed in bold caps under your return address. If your debtor put in a mail forwarding order you'll get the forwarding information back in the mail usually in less than 21 days.
- Look at the drivers license address. I'm aware that here in Texas if your license is suspended you have to obtain an ID card. So, search for your skip by name and date of birth to make sure you have covered that base, just in case.
- Looking for family that owns their home. Property records can help you locate those. I'm pretty sure my mom always knows how to get me on the phone, even if she doesn't know exactly where I'm at the moment.
- Professional license check. Every state has a different way of governing state licenses. Here in Texas electricians have their own website where they must register, insurance adjusters and sales have a different governing office and it's the same thing for hair dressers, real estate, doctors and nurses. If your skip has worked in a vocation, check to see if there is a license for that, it could yield a new address.
- Social media. As I've said before, we have moved from a "I did this, look see" to a "I'm doing this right now, look see" society. Free sites such as www.pipl.com scrub the internet for your skip giving you every possible link to the skips name.
- Is your skip self employed? Look for information on the BBB website. A complaint filed could get you a new lead.

- Warrants. In most counties and cities online site people can log on with their drivers license number and pay their tickets. Some information that may come up when looking for tickets to pay could be a new address (that was provided at the time of receiving the ticket) or phone number. Both the City of Houston and Harris County have online searches that show hot checks, traffic tickets and failure to appear cases that are closed. Those records provide older addresses that could be family homes. The addresses can be investigated in other ways to discover new associates (or X's that will spill the beans).
- Know what your skip is driving? Check for new vehicle registration, take note of when the registration expires and carfax.com will tell you the last time the auto has a state inspection. I've successfully called DOT and received the information of where the inspection station was, and made contact with the station requesting any information on file. Also, check the tow line in your county and city to see if it has ever been towed. You might get a nice surprise with a address or locate the unit in storage waiting to be picked up.

I'm sure that you already have a laundry list of things you already search for, new telephone numbers, addresses, place of employment, forwarding address, motor vehicles, insurance, court dates, etc…

We are all experts of hard to find skips. Having access to credit reporting agencies and as well as numerous other solutions to locate your skip and give you the professional edge by giving your client verified information is what sets you apart from all the rest.

Knowing how to skip trace is good for anyone. It's a new career; it boosts your self-employed income. It's awesome to learn new things. If something happens to me and I'm unable to work a full time job for someone else, I know how to find people. That skill is something that you can take to the bank.

The following is a conversation I had with Sandy G. in response to a post about learning to skip trace in a collection forum on LinkedIn. Sandy is a licensed P.I. in Florida and has years of experience in law enforcement. She thinks that all skip trace work should be done by a licensed private investigator in all 50 states. I did try to set her straight. So many different professions need skip tracing know-how to do a good job. Private investigators and debt collectors are only two jobs in which knowing how to locate someone is a large part of doing that job.

~*~

Sandy G. • A better choice would be to hire a licensed private investigator who specializes in person locates. These professional investigators have access to private databases that are FDCPA, GLB, FCRA, and FTC compliant not relying on sites such as Spokeo who received a heavy fine in June of this year to settle a FDCPA suit. (http://www.ftc.gov.) Most have years of investigative experience thus know how to search court records, etc. to find the debtor or the property your are looking for within the confines of the law. Some states, such as Florida, require a license to search for persons or property.

Note: Searching court records is something anyone can do at the court house in person. Court records are free public information but your county may not have an online retrieval system for family law fililngs or criminal records.

Valerie McGilvrey • It would not be a better choice to hire a license private investigator.

In the collections arena every collector must develop his or her own skip trace skills to locate debtors and collect their assigned accounts.

Collection agencies must have access to extremely fresh data. If you apply for credit today with a brand new address, I will have that address tomorrow.

Spokeo did get hit with a lawsuit, I read the article. But, they are still up and running and they still have good searches for reversing email addresses, IP addresses and other social media tracking related inquiries.

I'm aware also, that collection agencies in Florida must have a licensed investigator on staff to do skip trace work. This is not the case in every state. Such as Texas. Here we can do investigative skip trace work for the purpose of collections without a private investigators license. Those requirements do vary state to state.

Sandy G. • The fact is that a licensed professional will conduct a proper search. Anyone can hang out a sign and profess to "skip trace" and have no concept of the laws or how to conduct a legal search leaving his clients open to FDCPA suits. Why do you think this is illegal in Florida and should be in the other 49 states.

Valerie McGilvrey • I'm not going to argue with you. There are many states that don't require specific licensing requirements for being a private investigator. Alaska is one, Missouri and until recently Colorado was another state. Knowing that, I could just simply hang a shingle and start a business as a private investigator.

But we are in the area of collection agencies here. I've skip traced for many years and for me it's legal. I've now owned my collection agency since 2006. Like I said, if you are skip tracing to collect a debt, it's allowed. Otherwise you may be charged with stalking.

I don't see collection agencies hiring private investigators to do what they can do better. Private investigators are for the private sector. Why do you think it's legal in 49 states and illegal only in Florida?

Sandy G. • Because Florida has it right? Skip tracing within the confines of the law is allowed true. For example a search has to be done on a compliant site. There are only one or two, Tracers being one requires a license. Read the laws...I've then we can discuss it.

Valerie McGilvrey • I am very well versed on the laws. Just because I'm not a licensed private investigator doesn't mean that I don't have to be compliant. I must have permissible purpose (which is to collect a debt). I get audited for every credit report that I obtain. I've accounts directly with Experian, Transunion and Equifax. So, when I'm looking for someone to collect a debt I either own the debt or it has been placed with me to collect or enforce a security interest (repossess collateral). I also report my delinquent accounts to credit.

I'm pretty sure I know my state laws about my business and I know a private investigator would not improve my collection costs, but raise them significantly. I'm insured and bonded and have never had a complaint filed on my company. I do in turn think you need to read some collection laws as well.

Marketing

I want to give you just a few details about marketing and web tools that I use to grow my business and stay organized. If you are self-employed or planning to be this section is for you. Simple marketing has helped me gain a good and growing client base. Most of my clients are independent dealers or finance companies in the United States. Getting your first clients is always a memorable event.

I drove up and down a major highway in Houston calling tote-your-note lots from the phone numbers on their road signs. I asked if they had any skips that no one else could find. The response on my cold calls was better than I expected.

I walked into to one car lot after another picking up paperwork. It wasn't too long before I had more work than I could handle. At that time, very few independent dealers knew about the databases that I had access to, and even though in later years some clients would have access to those databases, many of my clients lost those databases due to new standards of outing abuse by auditing the searches by each user. Experian, Equifax and Transunion now asked for documentation of the debt owed by the consumer whose file was accessed. If another person's information had been accessed the account was shut down immediately.

I wanted to reach every single dealership in the Houston Yellow Pages. Looking into professional printing of postcards, I found Vistaprint.com had a deal for 100 free post cards (they still do, just Google "100 free postcards"), and I designed my own in just a few minutes. Post card stamps were a bit more affordable that year, and I got every single one of the 2,000 used-car dealers in Houston and the surrounding area. The test mailer was a smashing success. The response was fantastic as well as the referrals I received from quite a few happy clients.

http://www.vistaprint.com

http://www.gotprint.com

The postcard is the best form of marketing that I've ever done. I received phone calls months after the postcards were mailed letting me know the dealerships kept my postcard and the competition was almost nonexistent in a city of over 4 million people.

More repossession agencies today have staff skip tracers that run accounts through databases all day and make demand calls for collateral. I've known skip tracers that work for repo companies have a very short employment life and swear to never return to skip tracing. This job can be for anybody, and the end results are good for you if you dedicate yourself to keep learning.

There are smaller mom & pop operations that will give me assignments when they have exhausted all efforts on their own. These repossession clients have put me in contact with finance companies which in turn have given my company all their skip trace and collection work in my area.

When advertising to process servers for skip tracing, look for your state's list of authorized process servers online. I did this and received a huge response because the type of information I've access to. Home office resources can be limited so if you offer fresher data, then you have just become a necessity.

Here is a list of web sites that have helped me with marketing my skip trace business and collection agency while getting my office organized:

- Myfax.com
- Manta.com
- Webs.com
- Vistaprint.com
- Gotprint.com
- Listyourself.net
- Checkcomposer.com
- Constantcontact.com
- Dialmycalls.com
- Contactify.com
- Ringcentral.com

Since now the rest of the world is online; closing cases on a high volume basis is much easier than ever before. Finding a resource for getting the information you need is at your fingertips. There is no more wild goose chase on the street with most net savvy searches (while there's an importance to knocking on a skip's door or other in-person snooping to verify an address). The internet holds keys to the high speed chase that always gets your man, and don't forget to rely on your instincts. To compute is to err, to be human is divine!

If there is anything that you need help with as a skip tracer, I would be more than happy to help you figure it out. Just send me an email to Valerie@mcgilvrey.com

My company is Asset Management Service and you can find me on the web at www.cellbust.com

Made in the USA
Lexington, KY
01 February 2015